5

Consumers

Animals use a lot of energy. But they cannot make their own food. Animals get energy by eating other living things. Animals are consumers.

Some animals eat plants. Animals that eat plants are herbivores. A grasshopper is a herbivore. Rabbits and deer are herbivores too.

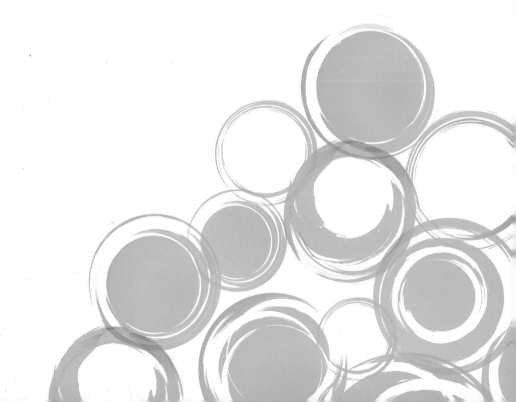

Some animals eat other animals.

They are called carnivores.

A frog that eats a grasshopper

is a carnivore. Can you think

of other carnivores?

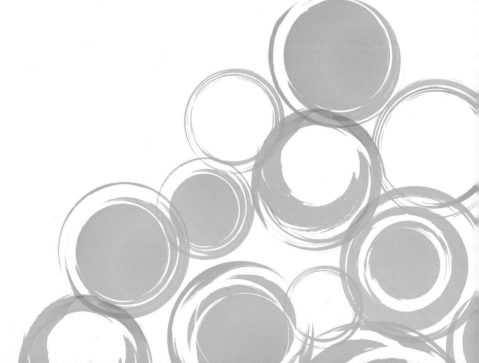

Some animals eat both plants and other animals. They are called omnivores. Bears, apes, and monkeys are omnivores. Can you think of other omnivores?

Decomposers

When plants and animals die,

they decompose, or rot.

Fungi and bacteria are decomposers.

They break down nutrients from

dead plants and animals.

Food chains

Plants and animals are connected
by food chains. A meadow
food chain starts with clover.
A grasshopper eats the clover.
Then a frog eats the grasshopper.

Producers

All living things need energy to live and grow. Plants are producers. They use energy from sunlight to produce, or make, their own food.

Contents

Food webs

Animals eat different kinds of things.
A grasshopper may eat clover
or grass. A bird or a shrew may
eat the grasshopper. Food chains
are connected in a food web.

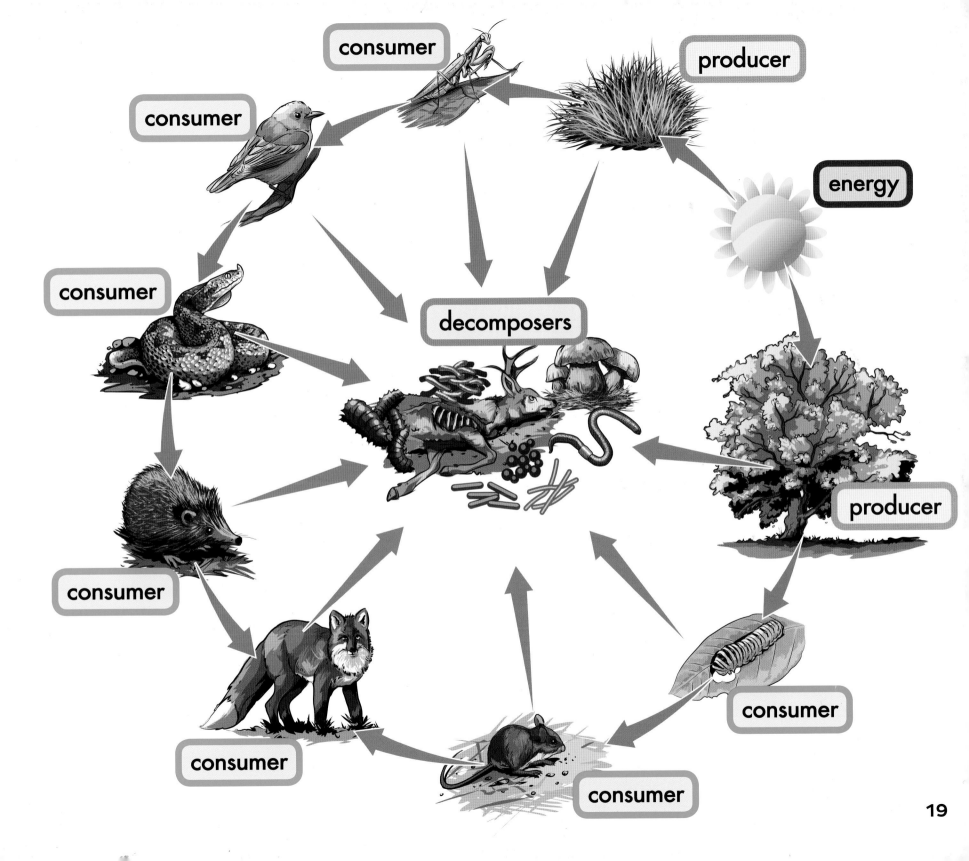

consumer

consumer

producer

energy

consumer

decomposers

producer

consumer

consumer

consumer

consumer

19

Activity

How do food chains form food webs? Make a model to find out.

What you need

- pencil
- index cards
- pieces of string
- tape

What you do

1. Write one of these names of plants and animals on each index card.

bean leaf	fox	sparrow hawk
blackbird	shrew	thrush
dead bean leaf	slug	
earthworm	snail	

2. Use these clues to make food chains.
   - shrews eat slugs, snails, and earthworms
   - slugs and earthworms eat plants
   - foxes eat shrews, blackbirds, earthworms, thrushes, and snails
   - sparrow hawks eat blackbirds and thrushes

3. Use the cards and string to make food chains. Tape the string from one card to another. Remember to start each food chain with a producer.

4. Use string and tape to join the chains at appropriate points to form a food web.

What do you think?

Make a claim.

A claim is something you believe to be true.

How do food chains connect to make a food web?

Use your model to support your claim.

Glossary

carnivore animal that eats only meat

consumer organism in a food web that eats plants or animals

decomposer small creature that feeds on dead plants and animals and turns them into soil

herbivore animal that eats only plants

nutrients parts of food that living things need to grow and stay healthy

omnivore animal that eats plants and other animals

producer living thing that make its own food from sunlight; grass and trees are producers

Find out more

Books

Food Chains (Fact Cat: Science), Izzi Howell (Wayland,2016)

Polar Bear: Killer King of the Arctic (Top of the Food Chain), Louise Spilsbury (Windmill Books, 2013)

Rainforest Food Chains (Food Chains and Webs), Angela Royston (Raintree, 2014)

Websites

www.bbc.co.uk/education/topics/zbhhvcw

Find out all about food chains and webs at this site.

resources.woodlands-junior.kent.sch.uk/homework/fooodchains.htm

This site explains the difference between food chains and webs.

www.sheppardsoftware.com/content/animals/kidscorner/games/foodchaingame.htm

This site has a game all about food chains.

Comprehension questions

1. What are animals that eat both plants and other animals called?

2. Animals are consumers. Explain what this means.

3. What do decomposers do?

4. What do you think would happen if there were no decomposers?

Index